# Special Services

For
Festivals and Occasions

Alan Dunstan

Kevin Mayhew

*TO*

*The Gloucester School for Ministry*

First published in Great Britain in 1991 by
Kevin Mayhew Ltd.,
Rattlesden, Bury St Edmunds,
Suffolk IP30 0SZ



ISBN 0 86209 197 7

Cover illustration by Lyn Ellis
Cover design by Graham Johnstone
Typesetting and Page Creation by Anne Hallam
Printed and bound in Great Britain by
J. B. Offset Printers (Marks Tey) Limited

# Contents

**Introduction** 5
**Acknowledgements** 6

**Carol Services: Advent, Christmas and Epiphany** 7
- **I Advent Carol Service** 8
- **II Christmas Carol Service** 10
- **III Epiphany Carol Service** 12

**Before and After Christmas** 15
- **IV The Road to Bethlehem** 16
- **V The Road from Bethlehem** 17
- **VI The Watch Night Service** 18
- **VII Good Friday Evening** 20
- **VIII I Am** 22
- **IX A Processional Service for Pentecost** 24
- **X A Simple Sequence for All Saints-tide** 26
- **XI Service of Praise & Prayer for the Creation** 30
- **XII Harvest Thanksgiving** 32
- **XIII A Birthday or Anniversary Service for an Organisation** 34
- **XIV An Outline Service of Thanksgiving** 36
- **XV Songs of Praise** 38

**Notes, Abbreviations** 40

# Introduction

This book is likely to be used mostly by Anglicans, though I hope that it may be of some value to others. The idea of devising services is still relatively new to Anglicans, and certainly belongs to this century. For the first half of it, some part of Evensong was usually *de rigueur* on Sunday evenings, and anything else that was wanted had to be added to it. But a carol service is now at least an annual event, and the 'family service' often occurs each month. There is no official liturgical provision for either; and there are many other occasions when some special form of service seems to be required.

*Patterns for Worship* suggests ways in which flexibility and creativity can be introduced without sacrificing structure in worship, or that balance of material which it always requires. In a 'special' service, not all the elements appropriate to a normal Sunday liturgy can be included. But such services must still have a structure if they are not to be a hotch-potch of assorted items. They should generally begin with recognition and worship of God, and end with a re-dedication to his service; and within them one item should naturally lead to another.

Anglicans have much to learn about liturgy from their fellow-Christians, and not least in the matter of hymnody. Many of the hymns suggested in the services will be familiar and easily available; reference is given to the sources in which they may be found, and I hope that what is less familiar will be seriously considered. Most of the services provide both for churches with choirs and those where the music is entirely congregational. No community should be asked to do things of which it is not capable; but every community should be encouraged to make full use of the resources available to it.

Acknowledgements

The publishers gratefully acknowledge the following for permission to reproduce copyright material in this book:

Church House Publishing, Church House. Great Smith Street, London SW1P for material from *Patterns for Worship* and *Promise of his glory*.

Every effort has been made to trace the owners of copyright material, and we hope that no copyright has been infringed. Pardon is sought and apology made if the contrary be the case, and a correction will be made in any reprint of this book.

# Carol Services: Advent, Christmas and Epiphany

The three services suggested here illustrate what I wrote in *The Use of Hymns**, and are an adaptation of those held in Gloucester Cathedral. Advent carol services have become increasingly popular in many churches; Epiphany carol services are less common, but, as I said in the book quoted above, could lift congregations from the doldrums into which they so often fall after Christmas. The services are linked by the contrasting movements of Advent and Epiphany, and by the way in which Scripture is used; the readings in Advent are mostly from the Old Testament, at Christmas from the Gospels, and at Epiphany from the New Testament letters.

The Advent service is obviously one of expectation. In larger churches, the first part could be held at the west end; during the hymn *O come, O come Emmanuel* or *The Advent of our God*, the choir and ministers move to the body of the church and occupy their usual positions, and during the hymn *Come, thou long-expected Jesus*, go to the sanctuary for the concluding part of the service.

The main movement of the Christmas carol service would be the procession to the crib – perhaps for its 'blessing' or, if that has already taken place, for prayers. Instead of a 'bidding prayer', prayers are offered at such points in the service as may be suggested by the readings or the movement.

For the Epiphany service, which has more simple anthems than carols, the movement could be in reverse order from that used at Advent. The Gospel would then be read at the altar, and the procession to the body of the church made during *As with gladness*. The choir and ministers would then process to the west end of the church during the hymn *Hail to the Lord's anointed*, and the remainder of the service would take place there and would symbolise the carrying of the light of Christ into the world.

Suggestions are made for both choral and congregational music, and alternatives are obviously possible. It is no less clearly important that there should be a recognisable link between what is read and what is sung, and that the musical items should be appropriate to the point in the service for which they are selected. A careful study of the choreography of the church should be made in order to see how the processions could be most effective. If there is no choir, perhaps the 'procession' could involve servers, churchwardens and minister, and in very small congregations, all those present might process.

* Kevin Mayhew 1990, page 60

# I Advent Carol Service

ENTRANCE

| | | |
|---|---|---|
| *Introit* | Choir | Matin Responsory *or* Advent Prose *or* This is the truth sent from above |
| | *or* All | The Lord will come and not be slow *or* O come, O come Emmanuel |
| *Reading* | Psalm 80. ASB version with three voices, reading respectively verses 1-2; 4-5; 8-19; all joining in the italicised refrain. | |
| *Hymn* | O come, O come Emmanuel *or* The advent of our God | |

PRAYERS

O Wisdom, Breath of the Most High,
pervading and permeating all creation,
**come, and make us friends of God.**

O Lord of Lords and Leader of the House of Israel,
who appeared to Moses in the burning bush
and gave him your law on Sinai,
**come and save us with your mighty arm.**

O Root of Jesse, standing as a signal to the nations,
before you all kings are silent:
to you the nations will do homage.
**Come and save us, delay no longer.**

O Key of David and Ruler of the House of Israel,
when you open, no one can close;
when you close, no one can open.
**Come and proclaim liberty to the captives**
**and set free the oppressed.**

O Rising Sun, Splendour of Eternal Light and Sun of Justice.
**Come and give light to those who live in darkness**
**and the shadow of death.**

O King of the nations, the Ruler they long for,
the cornerstone binding all together,
**come and save the people you fashioned**
**from the dust of the earth.**

O Emmanuel, our King and our Lawgiver,
the Anointed of the nations and their Saviour,
**come and save us, O Lord our God.**

LESSONS AND CAROLS

| | |
|---|---|
| *Reading* | Isaiah 40: 1-11 |
| *Carol* | People look East |
| or *Hymn* | Hark! the glad sound |

| | |
|---|---|
| *Reading* | Isaiah 11: 1-9 |
| *Carol*<br>or *Hymn* | The noble stem of Jesse<br>God is working his purpose out |
| *Reading* | Malachi 3:1-6; 4:1, 2 |
| *Carol*<br>or *Hymn* | Remember O thou man<br>Lo! he comes with clouds descending |
| *Reading* | Micah 5: 2-4 |
| *Hymn* | Come, thou long-expected Jesus |

PRAYERS

In joyful expectation of his coming to our aid,
we pray to him.
**Come, Lord Jesus.**

Come to your Church as Lord and Judge.
We pray for . . .
Help us to live in the Light of your coming,
and give us a longing for your rule.
**Come, Lord Jesus.**

Come to your world as King of the nations:
We pray for . . .
Before you rulers will stand in silence.
**Come, Lord Jesus.**

Come to your people with a message of
victory and peace.
We pray for . . .
Give us the victory over death,
temptation and evil.
**Come, Lord Jesus.**

Come to us as Saviour and Comforter.
We pray for . . .
Break into those areas of our lives
where we live with failure and distress,
and set us free to serve you for ever.
**Come, Lord Jesus.**

Come to us from heaven with power and great glory,
to lift us up to meet you with all your saints and angels,
to live with you for ever.
**Amen.**

CONCLUSION

| | |
|---|---|
| *Reading* | (3 voices) Isaiah 52: 7-10; Matthew 25:1-13;<br>Revelation 19:5-9 |
| *Hymn* | Sleepers, wake! (The chorale prelude might<br>be played and/or a verse sung by the choir) |
| *Blessing* | |

# II Christmas Carol Service

| | |
|---|---|
| *Introit* | Silent Night *or* Once in royal David's city vv 1 and 2 |
| *Reading* | Luke 1:26-38, the annunciation to Mary |
| *Carol* | Choir or All The angel Gabriel |
| or *Hymn* | Of the Father's love begotten |
| *Reading* | Matthew 1:18-25, the annunciation to Joseph |
| *Carol* | Joseph was an old man |
| or *Hymn* | To us a child of royal birth |

*Prayers*

Blessed be God, who in his love stooped to redeem mankind.
**Blessed be God for ever.**

Blessed be the King who made himself poor to enrich the needy.
**Blessed be God for ever.**

Blessed be the holy child who was born of the Virgin Mary.
**Blessed be God for ever.**

Blessed be the eternal Word who was made flesh for us.
**Blessed be God for ever.**

Blessed be Jesus, our Saviour and our Lord.
**Blessed be God for ever.**

| | |
|---|---|
| *Reading* | Luke 2:1-7, the journey to Bethlehem |
| *Carol* | O little town of Bethlehem |
| *Reading* | Luke 2:8-14, a heavenly host appears to the shepherds |
| *Carol* | Shepherds in the fields abiding |
| or *Hymn* | While shepherds watched |

Glory to God in the highest,
**And peace to his people on earth.**

Lord, we hear the angels' song of peace
in the fear and violence of our world,
and amidst its brutality and bloodshed.
Transform the deep longing for peace
into new resolution to seek justice and reconciliation,
and to guide and inspire the leaders of all nations.
**Give us, O Father, peace in our hearts,**
**that we may create peace in our homes,**
**and help to spread peace in the world. Amen.**

*Hymn, in procession to the crib*
It came upon the midnight clear[1]

*Prayers*

God our Father,
on this night we remember that your Son Jesus Christ
was born of the Virgin Mary for our salvation;
bless this crib which we have prepared to celebrate that holy birth;
may all who see it be strengthened in faith,
and receive the fullness of life which he came to bring,
who lives and reigns for ever. **Amen.**

Son of Man, our friend and brother,
you were born in a stable,
because there was no room in the inn.
While we celebrate your birthday
in the comfort of our homes this Christmas,
we remember the homeless, the hungry,
and all who are lonely or afraid.
Give us understanding of their need,
show us what we can do to help,
and make us generous in our love and gifts,
because of Bethlehem, because of your love for us all. **Amen.**

Lord Jesus Christ,
you were born among the creatures,
and your coming tells us again
that the whole created order is sacred;
help us to value and use wisely the resources of the earth;
give us gratitude for the natural order,
and compassion and care for all living things.
We ask this in your name. **Amen.**

*Reading* John 3:16-21, the message of God's eternal love

*Carol, as procession returns from crib*
See amid the winter's snow

*Reading* St John 1:1-14, the wonder of the Incarnation

*Hymns* Hark! the herald angels sing
O come all ye faithful (selected verses)

Lord, your son seems so small and vulnerable
as he enters the world at Christmas,
and yet we know that people from all races
have come to recognise him as King of Kings and Lord of Lords.
**Accept the worship and devotion that we bring in his name;
and use us to further the kingdom of love
which he came on earth to establish, for his sake. Amen .**

*Blessing*

# III Epiphany Carol Service

| | |
|---|---|
| *Introit* | Brightest and best[2]<br>*or* Whence is that goodly fragrance flowing |
| *Reading* | Matthew 2:1-11 |
| *Hymn* | As with gladness, men of old |
| *Reading* | Galatians 4:4-7 |
| *Anthem* | The holy child[3] |
| or *Hymn* | Let earth and heaven combine (HP 109) |

*Prayers*

Father, we thank you for giving your son to the world,
and for revealing his glory, not only to your chosen people
but to nations which did not know you.
**Let heaven and earth rejoice!**

You sent him to proclaim good news to the afflicted,
and liberty to the captives,
and to declare a time of grace, pardon and peace.
**Let heaven and earth rejoice!**

You led wise men by the light of a star,
so that they might offer to him their gifts
with their homage and their worship.
**Let heaven and earth rejoice!**

You call men and women to follow after them,
from the darkness into your wonderful light,
so that at the name of Jesus every knee should bow.
**Let heaven and earth rejoice!**

Enlightened by your grace and guided by your gospel,
we offer to your son, the treasures of our faith,
our hope, and our love, and the homage of a faithful life.
**Let heaven and earth rejoice!**

| | |
|---|---|
| *Anthem* | Myrrh, frankincense and gold[4] |
| or *Hymn* | Joy to the world! (HP 77) |
| *Reading* | Philippians 2:5-11 |
| *Anthem* | The Shepherds' Farewell[5] |
| or *Hymn* | All praise to thee, for thou, O King divine |
| *Reading* | Ephesians 2:11-22 |
| *Anthem* | From the rising of the sun |
| or *Hymn* | Hail thou source of every blessing |

*Prayers*

Let us pray for men and women of many faiths,
and for all who seek for truth and search for God.

For those by whose research the quality of life may be improved
and the environment protected.

For all who seek fairness and justice in our society,
the maintenance of good order,
and the constructive treatment of criminals.

For all who work for reconciliation among peoples
and so for the peace of the world.

And for ourselves:
**Lord help us to be honest in our search for truth,**
**obedient to the truth which we have received,**
**joyful in the truth that we proclaim,**
**for Christ's sake. Amen.**

*Hymn* Hail to the Lord's anointed

*Reading* Colossians 1:12-20

Choir or All Nunc Dimittis

*Responsary*

Send us to bring help to the poor
and freedom to the oppressed.
Father, by your Spirit,
**bring in your kingdom.**

Send us to tell the world the good news of your healing love.
Father, by your Spirit,
**bring in your kingdom.**

Send us to those who mourn, to bring joy and gladness
instead of grief
Father, by your Spirit,
**bring in your kingdom.**

Send us to proclaim that the time is here
for you to save your people.
Father, by your Spirit,
**bring in your kingdom.**

*Hymn* We have a gospel to proclaim
*or* Hills of the north, rejoice[6]

*Blessing*

# Before and After Christmas

When should *the* carol service be held? Christmas Eve would seem to be ideal; this is the time favoured by cathedrals, and might be possible in those very few parishes which do not have a midnight Eucharist. But where the midnight Eucharist is central to the Christmas celebrations, a full-scale carol service early in the evening would be impracticable, though a crib service is becoming increasingly popular. Liturgically, the carol service should not be earlier than Christmas Eve, since it then impinges on the proper observance of Advent. But, psychologically, this is wrong for most people. There have been carols for weeks, school services, nativity plays and the like, and Christmas really does seem to come to an end when the statutory holiday is over. Even when Christmas Day falls late in the week, it is alleged that people will not come to a carol service on the following Sunday. Nevertheless, there are parishes which hold out for this, with varying degrees of success; and there are instances where a carol service on St John's Day (or even in the late afternoon or early evening of Christmas Day) has been popular, because people are glad to have somewhere to go!

Another alternative would be to have two carol services, on the Sundays before and after Christmas. In the two related services offered here, 'The Road to Bethlehem' looks forward to Christmas, and 'The Road from Bethlehem' reflects on what happened at Christmas. The first service uses, in the main, Advent readings and hymns, but concludes with Luke 2:1-7, thus ending with more of a Christmas flavour than the purists would allow. The second service uses hymns and carols less likely to be sung on Christmas Day itself, and seeks to point us forward; this would be the more noticeable if *A stable lamp is lighted* could be chosen at the end. Choral items could be substituted for those suggested here, but the service is planned in such a way that it could meet the needs of churches without choirs, and relatively small congregations. But there probably will be some irregular churchgoers present; and provision is made in each service for a short address.

# IV The Road to Bethlehem

PREPARATION

*Sentences; Welcome*

*Hymn* O come, O come Emmanuel

*Prayers of Approach*

THE EXPECTATION OF THE MESSIAH

*Reading* Jeremiah 23: 5-6, the fulfilment of Israel

*Hymn* Come, thou long-expected Jesus

*Reading* Isaiah 11: 1-9, the goal of wisdom

*Psalm 19*

*Reading* Isaiah 35: 3-10, the answer to human need

*Hymn* Hark! the glad sound

*Reading* Isaiah 52: 7-10, the hope of the world

*Hymn* Hills of the north, rejoice

THE ROAD TO BETHLEHEM

*Reading* Micah 5: 2-4, the promise

*Hymn* Long ago, prophets knew

*Reading* Luke 1: 26-38, the annunciation

*Magnificat*

*Reading* Luke 2: 1-7, the journey

*Hymn* O little town of Bethlehem

THE MODERN PILGRIM

*Address*

*Carol* See him lying in a bed of straw (HP 118)
or *Hymn* Thou didst leave thy throne

*Prayers of Intercession*

*Hymn* O come, all ye faithful (omitting last verse)

*Blessing*

# V The Road from Bethlehem

ADORATION

*Sentences; Welcome*

*Hymn* Angels from the realms of glory

*Reading* John 1: 14-18

A short period of carol-singing may be introduced at this point, using items not in this service: perhaps around the crib.

*Prayers of Thanksgiving*

*Hymn* God from on high hath heard
*or* Joy to the world (HP 77)

THE INCARNATE LORD

*Reading* Luke 2: 21-28, the fulfilment of Israel

Choir or All Nunc Dimittis

*Reading* 1 Corinthians 1: 18-25, the goal of wisdom

*Hymn* Where is this stupendous stranger

*Reading* Luke 4: 16-21, the answer to human need

*Carol* Good Christians all, rejoice (HP 104)
*or* All my heart this night rejoices (HP 91)

*Reading* Colossians 1: 13-20, the hope of the world

*Hymn* The race that long in darkness pined

THE ROAD FROM BETHLEHEM

*Reading* Matthew 2: 12-23

*Carol* Unto us a boy is born

Or *Hymn* Glory be to God on high (HP 101)

THE MODERN PILGRIM

*Address*

*Hymn* O may we keep (last 2 vv of Christians awake)

*Prayers of Dedication*

*Hymn* A stable lamp is lighted[7]
*or* A great and mighty wonder

*Blessing*

# VI The Watch Night Service

Now that the midnight Eucharist has become almost universal at Christmas, the once-popular Watch Night Service on New Year's Eve is quite rare. But there are churches where it is held, and there are people who prefer this to any other way of 'seeing in' the New Year. The appended form of service could be held in a church, but also in a smaller and more informal atmosphere – perhaps in a home. It should not last more than 30 minutes, and might be only twenty, according to circumstances and the length of the address. The service traditionally ends just after midnight, and is one that must therefore be most carefully timed. Of the rich resources available in older books, the greatest treasure is perhaps Charles Wesley's hymn *Come let us anew*. Neither words nor tune are much known outside Methodism, and five minutes before the service could profitably be spent in learning them.

*Sentences; Welcome*

*Hymn of Adoration* Sing to the great Jehovah's praise (HP 360)
*or* Great God, we sing that mighty hand (HP 356)

*Prayers of Thanksgiving and Penitence*

*Reading; Address*

*Hymn* Select as appropriate to the Reading and Address

*Prayers of Intercession and Commitment*

In a world of change and hope,
of fear and adventure,
faithful God,
**glorify your name.**

In human rebellion and obedience,
in our seeking and our finding,
faithful God,
**glorify your name.**

In the common life of our society,
in prosperity and need,
faithful God,
**glorify your name.**

As your Church proclaims your goodness
in words and action,
faithful God,
**glorify your name.**

Among our friends
and in our homes,
faithful God,
**glorify your name.**

In our times of joy,
in our days of sorrow,
faithful God,
**glorify your name.**

In our strengths and in our triumphs,
in our weakness and at our death,
faithful God,
**glorify your name.**

In your saints in glory
and at the day of Christ's coming,
faithful God,
**glorify your name.**

*Hymn* Come let us anew (HP 354)

*Blessing*

# VII Good Friday Evening

In parishes where the worshippers have been free to attend church during the day, there will be little need for any special act of worship on the evening of Good Friday. If further devotion is required, *Evening Prayer* or *Night Prayer* (LHWE) with the appointed readings will meet such a need. And there are some churches where it is traditional to have special music on Good Friday evening, and others where an ecumenical service is usual at this time.

But many people have to work on Good Friday. If this involved the majority of the congregation, the main liturgy might be held in the evening, and in multiple parishes, one church might have it at this time.

The order of service suggested here is intended for those churches where most people have been able to worship during the day, but a substantial number have not. The service is therefore a reflection on the events of the day, with parts of the liturgy included in a sequence of readings. I have assumed an entirely congregational service, with hymns as the only music. But the canticles could, of course, be sung, and anthems, songs or instrumental music be added, or used instead of some of the material offered here.

THE CROSS FORESHADOWED

*Hymn* Praise to the holiest in the height

*Reading* Isaiah 52: 12-53:12

*Canticle* A Song of God's grace (Ephesians 1:3-10)[8]

*Prayer of Adoration* (LHWE p. 211, 1; Section 17)

THE CROSS DESCRIBED

*Canticle* Saviour of the world (ASB)

*Reading* John 19: 17-37

*Hymn* O sacred head[9]

*Prayer of Confession* The Reproaches (LHWE pp. 207-210)

## The Cross Interpreted

*Hymn* Nature with open volume stands

*Reading* Hebrews 10: 1-25

*Canticle* Song of Christ's glory (ASB)

*Prayers of Intercession* (LHWE pp. 212-216)

## The Cross Proclaimed

*Canticle* Glory and honour (ASB)

*Reading* 1 Corinthians 1: 18-25

*Hymn* Soldiers of the cross, arise

*Act of Affirmation* (LHWE p. 207 section 14)

# VIII I Am

A sequence of readings for the Easter season, incorporating five of the 'I am' sayings from St John's Gospel. In Year 2 some of these have been read in the Gospel at the Eucharist.

PRELUDE

*Introduction*

*Hymn* The God of Abraham praise

*Reading* Exodus 3: 7-14

PRAYERS

Let the voice of God's praise resound;
he is the source of our life.
**Let the voice of God's praise resound;**
**he is the source of our life.**

Be joyful in God, all you lands;
sing the glory of his name.
**He is the source of our life:**

Come now and see the work of God;
how wonderful he is to all people.
**He is the source of our life.**

Glory to the Father, and to the Son, and to the Holy Spirit.
**Let the voice of God's praise resound;**
**he is the source of our life.**

I AM THE LIGHT OF THE WORLD

Choir Hail, gladdening light[10]

*Reading* John 8: 12-19

*Hymn* Christ is the world's light, he and no other

*Collect* Eternal Light, illuminate us; eternal Power, strengthen us; eternal Wisdom, instruct us; eternal Mercy, have pity on us; and grant us with all our hearts and minds to seek your face, and to love your name, through Jesus Christ our Lord. **Amen.**

I AM THE BREAD OF LIFE

Choir Ave verum corpus[11]

*Reading* John 6: 30-51

*Hymn* I am the bread of life (HOAN 207)

*Collect* Lord Jesus, in the sacrament of your body and blood, you have given us a way to remember both your sacrifice for us and your presence with us. May we receive your salvation in all its fullness, and give ourselves to the service of others, to the praise of your great name. **Amen.**

I am the Good Shepherd

Choir Psalm 23[12]

*Reading* John 6: 30-51

*Hymn* Jesus the good Shepherd is (HP 263)

*Collect* God of peace, who brought again from the dead our Lord Jesus Christ, that great shepherd of the sheep, by the blood of the eternal covenant, make us perfect in every good work to do your will, and work in us that which is well-pleasing in your sight, through Jesus Christ our Lord. **Amen.**

I am the Way, the Truth and the Life

Choir Come, my way, my truth, my life[13]

*Reading* John 14:1-11

*Hymn* Thou art the way

*Collect* Lord Jesus Christ, the Way, the Truth and the Life; let us not stray from you, the Way, nor distrust you, the Truth, nor rest in any other but you, the Life; teach us by your Holy Spirit, what to believe, what to do, and wherein to take our rest; for we ask it in your name. **Amen.**

I am the Resurrection and the Life

Choir This joyful Eastertide (or another carol)

*Reading* John 11: 17-27

*Hymn* Now is eternal life

*Collect* Almighty God, whose Son is the resurrection and the life of all who put their trust in him; raise us, we pray, from the death of sin to the life of righteousness, that we may seek the things which are above, where he reigns with you and the Holy Spirit, one God, now and for ever. **Amen.**

Postlude

*Reading* Revelation 1: 9-19

*Hymn* Christ is alive! (HP 190)

*Blessing*

You believe that Jesus has been raised from the dead in glory.
**Amen.**

You believe that you have been raised with Christ.
**Amen.**

May your hearts and minds be set on things above,
and may those things inspire your life on earth,
and the blessing of God, Father, Son and Holy Spirit
be with you always.
**Amen.**

# IX A Processional Service for Pentecost

Much of this service takes place out of doors, and obviously has to be adapted to local circumstances – not least to traffic conditions. There is a paucity of choral music for this season, but suggestions are made for choir items where they are possible and practicable. The congregation might sing as it walks, and for this such songs and choruses as *The Spirit lives to set us free* or *Spirit of the living God* might be used.

IN CHURCH: ACT OF PRAISE

| | |
|---|---|
| *Introit* | Choir *or* All Veni Creator |
| or *Hymn* | Lord God, the Holy Ghost |
| *Reading* | Acts 2: 1-11 |
| *Hymn* | On the day of Pentecost<br>*or* Upon the day of Pentecost (HP 328)<br>*or* Our Lord, his passion ended |

*Prayers*

Spirit of God, present in creation,
bringing order out of chaos,
giving life to all things,
and sustaining them all in being,
**we give you praise and glory.**

Spirit of God, present at the new creation
when the Word was made flesh
and Jesus was born,
**we give you praise and glory.**

Spirit of God, present at his baptism,
and in his life and ministry,
**we give you praise and glory.**

Spirit of God, present with the disciples
on the day of Pentecost,
and with the servants of Christ at all times,
**we give you praise and glory.**

Spirit of God, present with us now to bring us to faith,
to fill us with love, and to unite us
in the fellowship of the church,
**we give you praise and glory.**

Spirit of God, Lord and giver of life,
**we give you praise and glory.**

Outside the church: the Spirit of mission

[Choir — Praise ye the Lord: Tye]

*Reading* — Acts 1: 6-8

*Hymn* — There's a spirit in the air

*Collect* — Almighty God, through whose grace we are called to serve you in the mission of the Gospel, and in the ministry of your love to all: bless us with the power of your Spirit, that we may be given courage, imagination and love in your service; through Jesus Christ our Lord. **Amen.**

At a school or college: the Spirit of wisdom

[Choir — If ye love me: Tallis]

*Reading* — John 16: 12-15

*Hymn* — Holy Spirit, truth divine

*Collect* — Lord give us wisdom that we may know what it is good for us to know, that we may do what you would have us do that we may be what you would have us be, in the name of Jesus Christ our Lord. **Amen.**

Outside another place of Christian worship: the Spirit of unity

[Choir — Ubi Caritas: Duruflé]

*Reading* — Ephesians 4: 1-6

*Hymn* — Filled with the Spirit's power

*Collect* — Spirit of promise, Spirit of Unity, we thank you that you are also the Spirit of renewal. Renew in your whole Church, we pray, that longing for your Kingdom which will unite us in one mission to the world, through him who prayed that we might be one, Jesus Christ our Lord. **Amen.**

Inside the other place of Christian worship: Act of dedication

[Choir — God be in my head: Walford Davies]

*Reading* — Galatians 5: 22-25

*Hymn* — O God, O spirit known to us (HP 309)
or God's Spirit is in my heart (HP 315)

*Prayers*

Spirit of life, source of all power and beauty,
**quicken our lives and renew our strength.**

Spirit of truth, illuminating the minds of men and women,
**reveal to us the hidden things of God.**

Spirit of Christ, witnessing to his grace and glory,
**Take possession of our lives, and make us more like him.**

*All join in the Grace*

# X A Simple Sequence for All Saints-tide

In view of the rich provision of resource material in *The Promise of His Glory* it may seem gratuitous to offer another service here; but as its title says, this is a *simple* sequence for All Saints-tide, and if it were desired, prayers from the above-mentioned book could be substituted for those suggested here. There is a plethora of good hymns for this season, and a fair amount of choral music is available so that alternatives for the hymns recommended here can easily be found; but I have tried to avoid the pitfall of choosing five or six hymns which all say much the same thing, and offer this comment as a warning!

ENTRANCE

*Scripture; Sentences*

*Hymn* Come, let us join our friends above (RS 472)

*Prayer* Eternal Father, from whom the whole family in heaven and on earth is named, unite us in our worship with all who are lifting up their hearts in prayer; that your whole Church thoughout the world, with the Church in heaven, may offer up one sacrifice of thanksgiving, to the praise and honour of your name. Through Jesus Christ our Lord. **Amen.**

THE SAINTS OF THE OLD COVENANT

*Reading* Ecclesiasticus 44: 1-15

*Hymn* We come unto our Father's God (HP 453)

*Prayers*

For Abraham, the father of the faithful,
**blessed be the Lord God of Israel.**

For the patriarchs, who succeeded him in faith,
**blessed be the Lord God of Israel.**

For Moses, who led your people to freedom and gave them the law,
**blessed be the Lord God of Israel.**

For the prophets, who heard and proclaimed your word,
**blessed be the Lord God of Israel.**

For David, and all who sang your praises of old,
**blessed be the Lord God of Israel.**

For those who in times of darkness, looked for the light,
**blessed be the Lord God of Israel.**

THE SAINTS OF THE NEW COVENANT

*Reading* Revelation 7: 9-17

*Hymn* Give me the wings of faith

*Prayers*

For the blessed Virgin Mary and the Holy family,
**glory to the King of saints.**

For the first disciples who left all to follow Christ,
**glory to the King of saints.**

For the apostles who carried the Gospel to many lands,
**glory to the King of saints.**

For Paul who interpreted that Gospel to the nations,
**glory to the King of saints.**

For the evangelists and writers of the New Testament,
**glory to the King of saints.**

For the messengers who brought
the good news to our own country,
**glory to the King of saints.**

For all those who have crossed boundaries in the service
of the kingdom and those who have given their lives in its cause,
**glory to the King of saints.**

## THE SAINTS IN OUR OWN LIFE

*Reading* Matthew 5: 1-12
*Hymn* Rejoice in God's saints *or* He wants not friends

*Prayers*

For the saints known to us
who have reflected your love in their lives,
**we thank you, Lord.**

For those who have influenced us, inspired us and helped us,
**we thank you, Lord.**

For all gracious people, whose presence has sweetened
and sanctified the world,
**we thank you, Lord.**

For the great company of every race and nation
who worship in your presence,
**we thank you, Lord.**

THE COMMUNION OF SAINTS

*Reading* Hebrews 12: 1-2

*Hymn* Ye holy angels bright

Homily

*Prayers*

Grant to us who are still in our pilgrimage,
and who walk as yet by faith,
that the Holy Spirit may lead us,
in holiness and righteousness all our days.
Lord we are your people,
**call us, guide us, keep us.**

May we have strength to meet the days ahead,
in joyful expectation of eternal life,
with those we love.
Lord we are your people,
**call us, guide, us keep us**

Help us, we pray,
in the midst of things we cannot understand,
to believe and trust in the communion of saints,
the forgiveness of sins,
and the resurrection to life everlasting.
Lord we are your people,
**call us, guide us, keep us.**

CONCLUSION

*The Lord's Prayer*

*Hymn* Glory to thee O Lord
*or* For all the saints

*Blessing*

# XI
# Service of Praise & Prayer for the Creation

This is an adaptation of a 'green' service drawn up by me for an RSCM diocesan festival. It could be used at various seasons of the natural year or for an organisation concerned with conservation.

Choir Let all the world in every corner sing[14]

*Introduction*

*Prayer* O God, most holy, most loving, infinite in wisdom and power: teach us to reverence you in all the works of your hand, and to hallow your name, both in our lives and in our worship; through Jesus Christ our Lord. **Amen.**

*Hymn* The spacious firmament on high *or* O worship the King

*Reading* Genesis 1: 1-2:3

*Psalm* 8[15]

*Reading* Job 38:1-12

Choir *or* All Benedicite

*Reading* From a Midrashic source.

And Isaac asked the Eternal: 'King of the world! When thou didst make the light, thou didst say in thy book that the light was good: when thou didst make the extent of the firmament and the extent of the earth, thou didst say in thy book that they were good; and every herb thou hast made and every beast, thou hast said they were good; but when thou hadst made man in thine own image, thou didst not say in thy book that man was good. Wherefore, Lord?' And God answered him: 'Because man I have not yet perfected; man is to perfect himself and the world'.

*Hymn* God in his love for us gave us this planet (HP 343)

*Prayers*

We pray for the world in which we live;
a world rich in resources,
yet exploited and laid waste
by humanity's lack of vision and respect.
Lord, as we rejoice in your creation,
**help us to give as well as to take.**

We pray for those with power and influence in the world;
for rulers whose policies pass sentences determining
the fate of their lands and those of other countries.
Lord as we rejoice in your creation,
**help us to give as well as to take.**

We pray for leaders in industry and commerce;
for those who farm and mine and fish;
for those who seek and make us aware
of the delicate balances within creation;
of the need for conservation and care.
Lord as we rejoice in your creation,
**help us to give as well as to take.**

We pray for all whose life is hard
because of the mystery of your creation
or the abuse of your gifts;
the victims of famine and disease,
of war and disaster.
Lord as we rejoice in your creation,
**help us to give as well as to take.**

We pray that we and all your people may be renewed in our faith
that you are creator and sustainer of the world;
help us so to live and minister to others that you may be seen
as a God of justice, wisdom and love.
Lord, as we rejoice in your creation,
**help us to give as well as to take.**

Help us to cling to the vision of your good purpose for all,
and so to pray for the redemption of creation,
when the world will see the true glory of your love,
made known to us in Christ. We ask this in his name.
**Amen.**

*Hymn* God you have given us power to sound

*Reading* Romans 8:18-25

*Hymn* Lord bring the day to pass (HP 347)

*Prayer* Awaken us, O God, to your presence, that we may walk in your world as your children. Give us reverence for all creation, that we may treat all living things with gentleness and all human beings with courtesy; through Jesus Christ our Lord. **Amen.**

*Blessing*

# XII Harvest Thanksgiving

Many parishes still have occasional worshippers at Harvest Thanksgiving, and are looking for a service directly related to the occasion. Here are some ways in which it could be planned.

PRAISE

*Prayer*
The earth is the Lord's and all that is in it,
**the compass of the world and those who dwell therein.**
The eyes of all look to you in hope,
**and you give them their food in due season.**

*Hymn* · Let us with a gladsome mind
or Come, ye thankful people, come

ACT OF THANKSGIVING

Perhaps this could be devised by a group, or different members assigned subjects such as:

i the created order,
ii the necessities of life,
iii the things we enjoy,
iv the people involved in all kinds of harvest,
v skills and inventions,
vi spiritual blessings.

Alternatively, the basis of a litany can be found in such books as *Companion to the Lectionary* Vol 3, Epworth (pp 192-193) or *New Every Morning*, BBC p. 79). In view of the occasion it is desirable that this should be a substantial part of the service.

*Hymn* We plough the fields
*or* Praise God for the harvest of farm and of field (HP 351)

MINISTRY OF THE WORD

This section could include lessons from the Old and New Testaments; Psalmody; the Benedicite or Song of Creation; perhaps non-biblical readings; anthem; sermon; hymns.

### The Presentation of Gifts

What is presented should be appropriate to the area concerned. In rural parishes, this is fairly obvious. In some urban parishes, gifts have been arranged under different headings such as 'gardens', 'shops' and 'overseas'. There may be individual members who can present some symbol of their own work. Symbols of spiritual nourishment – bread, wine and water, could be offered. The presentation could be in silence, with music, with scriptural texts, or with a brief statement by the presenter.

*Hymn* Lord of all good, our gifts we bring to thee
*or* To thee, O Lord our hearts we raise

### Act of Intercession and Dedication

A wide selection of prayers for the right use of natural resources and a fair distribution of them may be found in most books. Or the group devising the Act of Thanksgiving could take the same subjects for intercession and dedication.

*Hymn* Praise and thanksgiving
*or* For the fruits of his creation

*Blessing*

# XIII A Birthday or Anniversary Service for an Organisation

When such an event is planned, it is usual for a group of people representing the organisation to meet the minister concerned with drawing up the service; but compilation of services by a group can be time-consuming, and often results in something over-long. It is better for one or two people to collate ideas, and then bring out a draft. Among the initial questions to be asked are:

1 What is the main purpose of the service?

2 What are the things for which the organisation wants to give thanks?

3 Are there particular items – readings or hymns, for example – that must be included because they have special associations for this organisation?

4 Who is the preacher? Has he or she suggestions for lessons, or some theme that needs to be reflected in the service?

5 Is there to be special music by a choir, or group or soloist? if so, what is to be sung?
(It is important to have this information at an early stage so that this special item can be given an appropriate place in the service).

6 Are there suggestions for hymns?
(It is useful to try to distinguish between what may be *generally* desired by the organisation, and what happen to be the'favourites' of its representatives).

7 Is there anything to be 'dedicated'?

8 Is the national anthem to be included?
(If so, it is usually better that this be sung at the very beginning of the service).

## An Outline of the Service

1 *Welcome and Introduction*
2 *Hymn of Praise*
3 *Act of Thanksgiving*

The Act of Thanksgiving will often be in Litany form, and if printed, the responses present no problem. If not, there must be a special bidding to evoke the response for example:

Let us bless the Lord.
**Thanks be to God.**

A variety of such responsive material may be found in *Patterns for Worship*.

4 *Readings and sermon*
interspersed with hymns or music related to them.

5 *Prayers*
obviously for this organisation, and for others
whose concerns are parallel.

6 *Act of dedication*

7 *Hymn of dedication*

8 *Blessing*

# XIV
# An Outline for a Service of Thanksgiving

This title is now more commonly used than 'memorial service'. And whereas the older style of memorial service was often a replica of the funeral service, this is neither necessary nor usually desirable for a service of thanksgiving. Of course circumstances vary, and there may be occasions when this is for particular reasons not only the public form of the funeral itself, but the only occasion when most of the family can say farewell. But the outline suggested here assumes that this occasion is quite distinct from the funeral, and that its main purpose is indeed to give thanks for the life of the deceased. Yet, as many of those present will not have been at the funeral, a commendation of the departed and a recognition of the fact of death should not be absent from the service.

The Service of Thanksgiving might be planned in three parts:

**1** ACT OF THANKSGIVING AND COMMENDATION

Here the person's particular gifts and service would be remembered perhaps in a series of biddings. This could conclude with a prayer like that of no.50 on p. 334 of the *Alternative Service Book* (rendered into inclusive language) or the 'commendation of the departed' on p.75 of the URC *Service Book*, 1989.

**2** A 'MINISTRY OF THE WORD'

At a Christian service, there should be at least one reading from the Bible but other passages from non-biblical sources could be included. They would obviously be readings that meant much to the person concerned, or those which in some way reflected his or her life. There would often be an address at this point.

**3** INTERCESSION AND DEDICATION

Intercessions, where appropriate, for the concerns and activities of the dead person could be made here. The service could appropriately conclude with a prayer like that at section 10 on p. 314 of the ASB, or section 3 on p. 308. Alternatively, there might be short readings in all three sections of the service – something on the hope of resurrection under **1**; something closely connected with the person being commemorated under **2**; and a reading expressive of our own pilgrimage under **3**. Hymnody and other music could be interspersed throughout the service. Personal considerations would largely determine the choice, but it is a good principle to relate the hymns or music to the part of the service in which they are to be used. And there is usually time to plan such a service with sensitivity and care.

# XV Songs of Praise

In *The Use of Hymns*, I suggested that the 'Songs of Praise' style of service might be used at Christmas and Easter, and indeed at many other festivals, and that the Sunday theme might on occasions be explored in hymnody. These four examples are meant to amplify those suggestions.

### Christmas

At carol services where there is a competent choir, the items appointed for the congregation are usually very restricted and all too predictable – and seem to be based upon the assumption that people do not know and cannot sing anything else. I do not think this is always well-founded; but a more informal carol-singing could bring in fresh material and enable greater participation. This list includes songs from Iona, one of the great Wesley hymns on the Incarnation, and carols originating from many different parts of the world. Not all the items might be required at one session, but some could be interspersed with more familiar material.

1 Before the world began (WGS VOL 1 P12)
2 Who would think that what was needed (WGS1 P46)
3 Glory be to God on high (HP 101)
4 Where is this stupendous stranger (AMNS 527)
5 From heaven above to earth I come (HP 100)
6 A stable lamp is lighted (See Note 6)
7 How dark was the night of his coming (AP 340)
8 See him lying in a bed of straw (HP 118)
9 Infant holy (AHB 103)
10 Thou who was rich beyond all splendour (AHB 101)

### Easter

Easter is rightly and increasingly being observed as a season rather than as a single day or even a week, but, if there is not to be much repetition, sections on the Resurrection in our hymn-books need to be expanded. Among the hymns listed below are some that approach the theme in a new and refreshing way.

1 All ye that seek the Lord who died (HP 188)
2 Easter glory fills the sky (CH 276)
3 Christ is alive! Let Christians sing (HP 190)
4 If Christ had not been raised from death (AP 746)
5 The Saviour died, but rose again (HP 233)
6 Now the green blade rises from the buried grain (AMNS 501)
7 When Easter to this dark world came (HP 200)

8 Fairest Lord Jesus (CH 375)
9 Ye humble souls that seek the Lord (AHB 217)
10 The Last Journey (WGS2 P100)

CHRIST THE FRIEND OF SINNERS (7 BEFORE EASTER)

The theme is here explored in hymns from different centuries and different parts of the Christian spectrum. Perhaps this could be an ecumenical occasion.

1 God is love: let heav'n adore him (AMNS 365)
2 Amazing grace (HP 215)
3 Sinners, obey the gospel word (MHB 326)
4 Just as I am, without one plea (AMNS 246)
5 What a friend we have in Jesus (HP 559)
6 There's a wideness in God's mercy (HP 230)
7 There in God's garden (AMNS 514)
8 With joy we meditate the grace (AMNS 530)
9 Oh, the love of my Lord (HOAN 395)
10 Lord God, your love has called us here (AMNS 489)

ENDURANCE (20 AFTER PENTECOST)

The theme could describe the service unless the material is sufficiently varied – and some biographical information about the authors might be helpful here.

1 Awake our soul, away our fears (AMNS 436)
2 Shepherd divine, our wants relieve (AMNS 228)
3 O happy band of pilgrims (HOAN 228)
4 Now I have found the ground wherein (HP 684)
5 Will you anchor hold in the storm of life? (HP 128)
6 How firm a foundation, ye saints of the Lord (HOAN 202)
7 Who would true valour see/He who would valiant be (AMNS 212)
8 One more step along the road I go (HP 746)
9 Fight the good fight (AMNS 220)
10 Lo, I am with you to the end of the world (WGS2 118)

# Notes

1 A more Biblical and realistic version of the last verse is found in some recent hymn-books e.g. HP 108.

2 If sung by a choir, there is a setting by Malcolm Archer in *With a Voice Of Singing* (Kevin Mayhew).

3 In *With a Voice Of Singing.*

4 In *Sing His Praise* (Kevin Mayhew).

5 Berlioz *The Childhood of Christ.*

6 See the version in recent hymn-books, e.g. AMNS, New English Hymnal.

7 This has so far not reached standard collections in Britain, but is found in recent American collections, for example *Hymnal 1982.*

8 Suggested in *The Promise of His Glory*.

9 HP 176 provides a translation that can be sung with integrity.

10 Setting by Charles Wood.

11 A variety of settings available for choirs.

12 Settings without number!

13 Settings by W. H. Harris and others.

14 Settings by Leighton, Vaughan Williams and others.

15 A responsorial version by Colin Mawby could be used.

**Abbreviations**

| | |
|---|---|
| AMNS | Hymns Ancient and Modern - New Standard |
| HP | Hymns and Psalms |
| CH | The Church Hymnary 3rd Edition |
| HOAN | Hymns Old and New |
| AHB | Anglican Hymn Book |
| AP | Anglican Praise |
| MHB | Methodist Hymn Book 1933 |
| LHWE | Lent, Holy Week and Easter |
| RS | Rejoice and Sing (the new hymn book of the URC, published at the proof stage of this book): could be consulted for other texts, especially if inclusive language is required. |
| WGS1 | Wild Goose Songs Vol 1 |
| WGS2 | Wild Goose Songs Vol 2 |

Some of the hymns mentioned may, of course, be found in collections other than those cited.